A Big Beautiful Amish Courtship

Hannah Schrock

Table Of Contents

For the beauty of the earth, for the beauty of the skies,
For the love which from our birth over and around us lies,
Lord of all to Thee we raise this our sacrifice of praise.

Martha King stood outside the dress shop waiting for Saloma to return. Saloma had tried to get Martha to come in with her but Martha refused, insisting that nothing in the store would fit her properly.

"You won't know unless you try Martha! Besides, you're not that big," Saloma had pleaded with her friend.

"It's not proper anyway Saloma, why do you insist on wearing such Englisch styles? You will be married to Samuel soon and will have to stop being so frivolous!" Martha scolded. Saloma was a lovely young woman, at nineteen she was a year younger than Martha, but they had been friends since infancy.

"It's my last chance to go to an Englisch dance which is why I am going to get the nicest Englisch dress I can. Within the month I will be baptized and married, so I might as well go a little crazy one last time."

Martha shook her head and Saloma smiled and dashed into the store. It wasn't that Martha disapproved; it was just that she sort of wished she was Saloma sometimes. Saloma was naturally thin with pretty blue eyes and blonde hair. Every boy in the community had wanted to court Saloma, while Martha could only sit by and watch. It made Martha sad and ashamed at her sin of covetousness. She quickly and silently prayed for forgiveness. As she was praying two teenage Englisch girls walked by, as they passed her they giggled to each other. They lowered their voices, but Martha could still hear their comments.

"I know the Amish have no fashion sense but that dress on that much fat makes her look like a whale." They both laughed and Martha blushed with shame.

Martha had gained a lot of weight since her father had passed. She knew he was in a better place but she still missed him terribly. She had turned to food for comfort and working in the family restaurant didn't help matters. Food was always around her and it never laughed at her or made mean comments. It knew how she was feeling. It could make her feel good when everything else seemed to be crumbling. Even after her mother, Emma had sold the family farm, furniture business and the restaurant, Martha's over eating didn't stop. She spent her mornings baking and her evenings eating the fruits of her labor. She didn't like going out anymore and spent most of her time at home. Her mother had tried to help but she didn't know how. The matter was left to grow. And grow Martha did.

Saloma finally returned from the shop with a bag held proudly in her hand. "I found the perfect dress! I look beautiful in it, you should have come in to see."

"I was happy waiting for you here and resting in the blessed sunshine of the day," Martha said but she didn't really mean it. She was trying to be bright and chipper for her excited friend, but it was hard. She felt sad and lonely but Saloma wouldn't understand. It wasn't a subject the two of them ever spoke about. The two young women made their way down the street to meet the two girls they had travelled into town with. When they were in sight Martha saw the girls pointing in her direction and whispering something to each other. She imagined that it wasn't very kind, but then that was always her first reaction. Assuming the worst. It was a poor trait and Martha vowed to pray on the matter and hoped she would find the strength to find the good in people. As the eldest Martha had brought them all in her family buggy. Miriam Fisher and Sarah Zook were both sixteen and had begged to come into town with the older girls. Martha had agreed as always and the company had been pleasant as they drove into town to do some shopping.

Martha had to go to the bank and she needed to pick up some material to make a new quilt for her mother. She had found some lovely floral prints that weren't too over the top. Plain was always best. While Saloma and Martha were selecting fabrics the teens had wanted to go and get ice cream, so they agreed to meet back at the buggy in an hour. Thanks to Saloma's trip to the Englisch dress shop they were already well past the hour mark.

"Are you ready to head home?" Martha asked the girls.

"Couldn't we go watch the baseball game at the high school?" Sarah asked, giving Miriam a knowing look.

"How do you know there's a baseball game at the high school today?" Saloma asked.

"We heard about it when we went to get ice cream."

"Really?" Saloma asked them with a frown.

The girls looked sheepish and finally Miriam spoke. "Ok, we knew there was a game. We met a couple of boys last Saturday night and they told us they played on the high school team. They're really cute, could we please go and see them play, just this once?"

Saloma was about to protest but Martha had already agreed. "They are only young once." Martha sighed. Saloma gave her a poisonous look but she knew that Martha would let the girls get their way, Martha always gave in to the wishes of others.

They spent over two hours at the baseball game. After the game had finished the girls said they just wanted to go over and congratulate the boys on their victory. Again Martha relented and Saloma grew angrier.

"You have to stop letting people trample all over you, Martha!" Saloma stated.

"I am not. They just want to talk to a couple of boys." Martha replied.

"Englischer boys!" retorted Saloma.

"Hang on. You are going to an Englisch dance this evening!" Martha argued.

"I've not just turned sixteen! I know how the world works!"

"OK, OK, we will bring them home now." Martha responded and started toward the girls. The two girls ran to Martha, their eyes bright with excitement and smiles beaming from their faces.

"They asked us to go for sodas, can we please?" Miriam begged.

Martha looked and Saloma and saw the anger rush to her cheeks. "I'm sorry we can't, Saloma has to get home." Martha said.

The girls fussed a bit but looking back at the boys shook their heads no. With glum faces they all retreated to Martha's carriage. The ride home was quiet and sulky. It seemed she had managed to upset everyone. If she was honest, it suited Martha just fine.

Isaac Yoder was busy working on his family's farm. He was the eldest of three boys and the only one yet to marry. At twenty-two his father had begun to put pressure on him to find a wife. Isaac wanted to court Rebecca Miller but he had never worked up the courage to ask for that all important buggy ride. Rebecca was just eighteen and the prettiest girl in the community. He knew if he didn't get the courage soon someone else would take her.

Church was next Sunday and he decided that this was his big chance. He had cleaned his buggy everyday and groomed the old horse, in anticipation. He kept practicing what he would say to her. He had prayed almost every minute of every day for the courage, and he hoped that it wouldn't fail him. Marriage season was fast approaching and he didn't want to wait another year to take a wife. To be twenty-three and still not married, would be tough. Especially when his younger siblings had already taken the step. He had been baptized three years ago. Back then he felt that Rebecca was too young to court, but she got to be so pretty in the last year that he felt his courage leave him. He had always known, somewhere deep inside that she was the girl he would marry. However, now was the time to make it happen and he just didn't know how.

Isaac was busy cleaning the tools and putting them away when his father came into the barn.

"Isaac, you worked hard today. You make me so proud," Jacob Yoder said, pacing his statement carefully. His compliment was soon followed by a question, "I was wondering if you have thought anymore about what we spoke of last week."

Isaac was dreading this conversation. "You mean about Martha King?"

"Yes of course. She is a lovely girl and she would make you a good match." Jacob said.

"I have already told you Daed, I am going to ask Rebecca Miller." Isaac tried to control his temper. His father and mother had been putting pressure on him for weeks to consider Martha King as a match, but he just wasn't interested.

"Rebecca is a pretty girl but she has no substance, Martha has substance." Jacob smiled.

"Ach, she has lots of substance Daed."

"Don not refute me, boy!" Jacob said a flash of anger in his voice.

"I am sorry Daed, but we have had this conversation before. I don't want to marry Martha. I hardly know her.

"You haven't even given her a chance Isaac. You have had your eye on Rebecca this whole time but you have never asked her to court. It's time you choose another. Face it, Rebecca is just not Gott's will." Jacob insisted

Isaac had grown tired of this discussion. He had been having similar ones about different girls, with both his parents for far too long. He knew why they were pushing Martha King on him. It was simply because her family had a lot of money. Even before Emma King had sold her husband's businesses Jacob had been encouraging his son's to consider Martha as a wife. With the marriage of each of his boys Jacob had become more and more desperate to have one of them marry a woman of wealth. Martha King was as about as wealthy as any in the community. He had offered them land, extra privileges, anything to get them to concede but none of them would. His last chance was Isaac and he would not let Isaac forget it.

"You must go in and get yourself cleaned up. We are going to the King's house this evening for a visit." Jacob announced and turned from Isaac before the young man could refuse.

Isaac's head dropped to his chest and he let out a great sigh. It was clear his father was not going to give up. He would have to appease him. He decided that he would go along with his father's tricks but he would find a way to make Martha refuse his courtship. If Martha refused him, there would be nothing Jacob could do to make a match, and Isaac could go back to concentrating on courting Rebecca.

But time was ticking. He wanted to get rid of the prospect of Martha before next Sunday.

Next Sunday after church he would not sit across the long table from Martha, he would sit across from Rebecca. They would talk as they always did and he would ask if she would like to go for a buggy ride. If it went well, he would ask for another. Then on the way home from that ride or maybe in her parents' house after the ride he would ask her to court. She would say yes and in a few weeks he would ask her to marry him. It would be quick, but he had been planning it for years If Martha were to reject him, Jacob would have no choice but to approve.

Isaac strode into the house. He would make himself presentable, but he would find a way to be mean to Martha. He wasn't normally a mean man, but he would do it for Rebecca. It would be hard, Martha was a really nice person, but he had to do it.

That evening Martha showed her Mother the cloth she had found for the quilt.

"It is lovely dochder," her Mother cooed. "You have such wunderbaar taste. You will make a man very happy."

Martha cringed. She knew what was coming next. It was the same old argument that had played out too many times before.

"You are getting old Martha, you should choose for yourself a husband," Her mother smiled, love escaping from every pore. Martha knew her mother adored her, but she just didn't understand. It wasn't that Martha hadn't tried to attract a boy, she had, but no one wanted her.

"Mamm, we have spoken of this before. What man would have a woman such as me?" Martha held her hands out to her sides to draw attention to her girth. "I am not attractive to the boys in the community."

"You are beautiful Martha. You could lose a little weight, I will give you that, but a little effort is all you need."

"I need to have peace from this subject." Martha retorted anger slipping off her tongue.

"You need to pray to Gott for forgiveness of your sins and to provide you a husband that you can rely on." Her mother responded, frustration clear in her voice.

"Mamm, I have prayed. I will pray again if it makes you happy. But if it is Gott's will that I am a spinster, at least he has provided the means to survive it." Martha spoke with conviction. She had convinced herself that it was true. She would always be alone but at least she wouldn't be destitute as well.

Her mother shook her head. "You think you know so much, but you don't. Yes you have means, but you need a man too. I know that there is such a man that has had his eye on you. You have not noticed a good looking man showing you interest?" her mother questioned with little sly a smile on her face.

"What man is this?" Martha demanded. She felt her stomach flip. Could it be true?

Was there someone that wanted to court her? Had she been so blind that she missed what she had hoped for most of all?

"Freshen yourself and warm a pie, we are expecting company in an hour," Emma smiled lovingly at her daughter.

"Who is it?" Martha asked, smoothing her dress unconsciously.

"Jacob, Ruth and Isaac Yoder," Emma grinned.

"Isaac Yoder?"

"Yes! He is a good looking man. Strong and he is a hard worker. He will make you a fine husband."

"But Isaac Yoder has his eye on Rebecca Miller, everyone has seen it."

"His father stopped by earlier today with some milk from his cows. He asked about you and confided in me that Isaac has always liked you and speaks of you with great fondness."

"That can't be right. Isaac and I barely speak to each other. We have no interest in each other, we aren't even friends."

"Maybe that is why you never noticed him looking at you? His father assures me that he would like to court you. Now go and make yourself pretty and warm that pie." Her mother insisted.

***

The pie was warm and Martha had tidied herself up. She couldn't believe what her mother had told her. There had to be some kind of mistake. Isaac Yoder was good looking. He was quite tall and had a muscular physic. Many of the young girls wanted to court him. Martha tried to imagine being his wife, but she just couldn't. Despite Isaac's good looks, she wasn't drawn to him. Martha knew that looks shouldn't be the basis of a relationship. She knelt at her bedside and prayed for guidance.

Martha rose and nervously straightened her dress. She didn't know what to make of all this, but she would obey Gott's will, even if it meant marrying Isaac Yoder.

When the Yoder's arrived Emma answered the door.

"Welcome to our home, come in come in," Emma chimed. Her excitement at welcoming guests, especially one who might become her son-in-law was evident in her tone. "Martha made pie for us to enjoy, please come in."

Martha brought out the pie and set it on the table. She looked up at Isaac and blushed.

"Martha, it is so good to see you looking so well." Jacob said, gesturing to his son.

Isaac tried not to smile. He would look mean even if he couldn't act mean. He took a seat at the top of the table away from everyone. He slumped in the chair and did his best to look sloppy and lazy.

Martha served the pie to everyone. She felt hot and uncomfortable, all eyes were clearly on her. She looked at Isaac for some reassurance but found none. She had never seen him acting this way. She didn't know him well but she had seen him in the community. He was usually a happy young man who carried himself with dignity. Today he looked like a sulky little boy who had his ball taken away. Jacob Yoder must be mistaken in what he told her mother.

The parents insisted that Martha join Isaac at the top of the table so that the young ones could talk. Martha reluctantly agreed and sat at the table across from Isaac.

"Do you like the pie?" She asked him politely.

"Not really," he lied, "the crust is too tough and tastes too salty and the apples are over cooked. Did you use any cinnamon? I can barely taste it over the salty crust." He prayed that Gott would forgive his sin. He felt sick saying such mean things but once he started he found it hard to stop. "Did you make that dress? It's a bit tight isn't it? Perhaps you should be more modest."

Martha felt her face go red. His words stung her and she couldn't help but lash back at him. "At least I know how to sit in a chair and speak politely when I'm a guest in someone's home. I suppose you forgot your manners at the door?"

He screwed up his face and mocked her. "Probably. I do it all the time. What will you do about it?"

Martha rose from the table and calmly went to her room. She offered no explanation. She didn't know what to make of this man who seemed to have lost his mind. It wasn't long before her mother followed her.

"You rude girl, you left Isaac sitting on his own." Emma chastised, her face like thunder.

"You weren't there. He was being rude to me. In fact worse than that. He said terrible things. So I left him to be rude to himself."

"Ach Martha, don't be so silly. He likes you. He was probably just nervous, you know how boys can be. You will have another chance tomorrow. We are going to their home for dinner."

Martha was stunned. Suddenly she realized that her mother and Isaac's parents meant to see the pair married. They didn't seem to care whether Martha and Isaac liked each other. For some reason it didn't seem to matter. Isaac didn't seem to be accepting of his parents plan. If he wanted to court Martha surely he would have been nicer? Could her mother be right? Could he just be nervous? Martha was doubtful that was the answer. She thought that maybe Isaac didn't like her and was being pushed into courting Martha the same way as Martha was being pushed into courting him. But that couldn't be right. He was a man. Surely he could stand up to his parents? The more Martha thought about it the more her head hurt.

Maybe Gott would have the answers?

Early the next day Martha went for a walk. Her mother had been so filled with joy at the thought of her and Isaac being a match that Martha decided she had to find a way to like this young man. Maybe he wasn't feeling well last night? That must have been the problem. She had seen Isaac around his friends before and he always seemed like a nice person. It must have been nerves or something that made him behave so badly.

Martha was deep in thought when she was suddenly crashed into by an English man heading in the opposite direction. The young man was as deep in thought, just as Martha had been and they didn't notice each other.

Martha laughed. "I am so sorry. I didn't mean to bump into you."

"It is completely my fault," the young man said smiling.

Martha noticed that he turned his head at a funny angle when he spoke to her. He was wearing a hoody pulled so far over his head that most of his face was in shadow. She saw redness around his forehead on the part of his face that he seemed to be trying to hide. Martha felt a pull in her stomach toward this sweet young man. "I'm Martha King," she offered by way of an introduction.

He glanced at her and a look of recognition flashed over him. He became fidgety and nervous. "I'm sorry, are you okay?"

"I'm fine" Martha replied with a smile. She tried to get a better look at him but he kept pulling the hoody further and further down until it nearly covered his whole face.

"Do I know you?" she asked quietly.

"I have to go," the man said nervously and skirted around her. He pulled at the hoody again doing his best to hide his face.

Martha was perplexed by the meeting. He looked familiar but she couldn't place him. She watched him go along his way, and as he disappeared into the distance he kept looking back at her. He was an Englisch boy, but she didn't know any Englisch boys. She turned and continued on her way, trying to place the face beneath the hood and trying to understand his reaction to her.

***

Eli Byler had been out early to pray and think. He had just come back to the community after a twelve year absence. When he had been eight years old tragedy had befallen his family. His father had lost his faith in Gott and rejected the community after then. He moved what left of his family far away and into the English world. Eli understood his father's pain, but not his rejection of Gott. Wasn't it Gott's will that this tragedy should have happened? There had to be a reason why Gott would allow this to happen. Wasn't there.

Eli thought of the heartbreak that had changed his whole life. He had been raised in this community and it was all he knew. Then one winter's night, everything changed.

Late at night. Flames engulfed the family home. Eli, his younger sister, and their father had escaped the flames. But their mother, and Eli's twin sister perished in the blaze. He had tried to so hard to save his twin that he nearly died as well. To this day he felt the guilt that his mother and sister had died and he had survived. His father had uprooted the family two months after the fire and brought them to Chicago. Eli suffered a culture shock that was devastating. Not only had he been physically disfigured, burns covered one of his arms and a quarter of his face, but mentally he felt adrift, alone and lost. His father put him into therapy where he learned that he was suffering from something called survivor's guilt. He received skin grafts and physiotherapy to heal his physical wounds but the scars, both internal and external remained.

Moving to the English world was the worst part. The other children made fun of his scars and the way he spoke. His father had quickly bought them new English clothing to wear, but he had bought the wrong kind and Eli was mocked for wearing "nerd" clothes. He did eventually make some friends, but they had become so obsessed about acquiring wealth that he could no longer relate to them.

His sister had fared better. She was only three at the time of the fire and didn't even remember the community she had been born into. Eli's father had remarried and his new wife raised his sister as her own, but it was never the same between Eli and his step-mother. It wasn't that he didn't like the woman, he did, but she couldn't replace the mother and community he had lost so long ago.

Now that he was an adult he could make his own choices. His father tried to convince him not to come back but Eli had felt the draw to return since the day he left. It was like a toothache that just wouldn't leave him. He tried to please his father, but it was no use. He wrote to his mother's sister who was still in the community and she welcomed him with open arms. Her children were mostly grown and married so Eli had been a welcome addition. The whole family celebrated his return as he imagined the prodigal son's return had been.

He was enjoying this life. He had only been here a week and he already felt at home. He hadn't made the transition to Amish clothing as yet. But it was coming in the near future. He was considering his baptism. The Bishop would take a while to allow it, he knew that. But baptism would mean that he could marry and he wanted a wife more than anything else. Yet there were numerous problems with that. Acceptance back into the community for one. His appearance for another. He had been meditating on this very subject when he ran, literally, into Martha King. Martha had been his best friend when they were young. They were inseparable as children. Martha's father told them a story called The Three Musketeers that he had heard once, a long time ago. He told the children that they were like those Musketeers, always together, always looking after one another. Eli flinched at the thought. He hadn't looked after his sister the night of the fire; at least not well enough to save her. His thoughts were brought back to Martha. Her eyes hadn't changed at all. She had a sparkle of pure kindness that had always been there. He wanted to run after her and throw his arms around her, tell her how much his memory of her had brought him comfort over the years, but he couldn't.

It wouldn't be proper for starters.

Would she even remember him?

Martha had been thinking of the young man she had run into earlier in the morning. She was sure she knew him but she still couldn't place him. Martha's mother, Emma had been fusing all day about this evening. The dinner at the Yoder's had become a huge event with what seemed to be almost half the community now attending. Martha didn't know how it had happened but it turned out that all of the Yoder's would be there, Isaac's brothers, cousins, aunts and uncles. The Fishers were coming along with the Lapps and several of the King's extended family. Martha was not looking forward to it in the slightest. She and her mother had started baking loaves a for the event as soon as Martha had returned from her walk, they may as well have ran a bakery. She had allowed herself to focus on her work so she wouldn't have to think about Isaac.

As afternoon turned into evening, they loaded the buggy with the produce and set off in the direction of the Yoder house. Such was her excitement that Emma did not notice her daughter's mood was that of doom and gloom.

"You will have a wunderbaar time my dochder! You will see. The Yoders are a good family. You will be blessed to be one of them," Emma almost sang.

"We haven't even begun to court Mamm. I don't think Isaac likes me. You didn't see the way he looked at me and you didn't hear how he spoke to me," Martha exclaimed.

"You will see Martha, it will be different today. Isaac will be with his family and he will not be nervous with them around him."

Martha decided not to argue. She knew her mother was too busy dreaming of her future grosskinner and when she started with that nothing could stop her.

"Ach, and Martha, you will never believe what else I have learned today!" Emma continued. "I was speaking with Hannah Fisher. You remember her sister died in that tragic fire so many years ago."

Before Emma could finish Martha shouted, "Eli!"

Martha sat up in her seat a smile of realization crossed her face and her heart leapt with joy.

"How did you know the boy was back?" Her mother muttered, disappointed that she didn't get to deliver the news.

"I ran into him this morning but I didn't recognize him," Martha's voice was filled with excitement. "Is he coming to the dinner tonight?" she asked.

"Jah, he is." Emma sounded annoyed. She didn't like the enthusiasm in her daughter's voice. Eli Byler had been in the English world for far too long. Emma had made a good match for her daughter. She would have to keep her eye on Eli Fisher.

At the dinner Martha kept looking for Eli but she didn't see him. Isaac had been trying to get Martha's attention most of the night but she had been distracted. They sat opposite each other during the meal but no matter how rude Isaac was to her, he couldn't get Martha to pay any attention to him. He stopped trying to be rude and started being his usual polite and friendly self. He still couldn't get her to notice. How could he get her to reject the match if she wasn't even paying attention?

After the meal Martha searched out Hannah. "Hannah, it's so nice to see you." Martha said as casually as she could muster. "I heard you have Eli staying with you. Is he here?" She hoped she didn't sound too obvious.

"No, he wouldn't come." Hannah said quietly.

"Why's that?"

Hannah paused for a second as if she were assessing the situation. Finally she began to speak. "His face. Out in the Englisch world people gave him a hard time about the scars. It seems that he fears rejection. As if people will see the scars and remember that he lived and the others died."

"I didn't notice them this morning." Martha said feeling slightly uncomfortable at mention of Hannah's dead sister.

"You saw our Eli this morning?" Hannah asked, surprised.

"Jah, we almost ran into each other. He didn't tell you?" Martha's heart sank. She wasn't sure if he hadn't recognized her or if he just didn't care.

"Ach that explains his mood this morning. When he got back from his walk he went out to the barn and has been there ever since working on who knows what. He said that he couldn't come tonight because he had too many things to think about," Hannah sighed.

"He has been away for so long and yet he is still the little Amish boy who I remember."

Martha smiled. She remembered that little Amish boy. She longed to see the man he'd grown into again. Isaac came and tapped her on the shoulder.

"Your Mother wants you," he told her. She smiled weakly and went to find her mother. Isaac was surprised, maybe he wouldn't have to work so hard to get her to reject him, and she seemed to be doing it without his encouragement.

Emma was furious with Martha. She had ignored Isaac the whole time and poor Isaac had been trying to get Martha's attention. This is why her daughter had never managed to get a husband, she was too distracted.

"What have you been doing? Isaac has been trying to get your attention all night and you are ignoring him, for what?" Emma whispered to her daughter, not wanting any of the other guests to hear.

"Ach, I didn't realize he was trying to get my attention. Mamm, Hannah says that Eli hasn't changed, he is not so Englisch after all."

Emma looked at the glow on her daughters have and grew concerned. "Stop thinking about this Eli and start thinking about Isaac. He is a good Amish man and he wants to court you. If you would only let him. Don't think of young Eli, it will only bring heartache when he goes back to the English world. I love you my dochder, don't let your heart be broken, I could not bear to watch it." Emma pleaded.

"Jah Mamm you are probably right. I will go and talk with Isaac," Martha conceded. She didn't know where Eli's heart lay, it was only a chance encounter after many years away. She only hoped that he intended to stay in the community.

It turned out the opportunity to talk to Isaac had already been lost because Jacob had started some games for the young folk. He made sure that Martha and Isaac would be paired up. The evening started with an energetic game of volleyball and then slowed down with a few board games. When everyone was tired and it was time to go home, Jacob told Isaac to offer to drive Martha home. Isaac frowned he had fun with Martha but he still wasn't interested in marrying her. He would offer to drive her home, but it wouldn't be a proper buggy ride. He had no desire to ask her if they could start courting. He would simply tell her the truth about their parents plans for them and then own his feelings for Rebecca. It was only fair.

Martha had agreed to be driven home by Isaac. He had asked right in front of Emma. Her mother stuck her elbow into Martha's back to push her into saying yes. She didn't have much of a choice.

"Did you enjoy your evening?" Isaac asked.

"Jah, it was quite pleasant, thank you." Martha said. She didn't feel close to Isaac at all. She hoped he wouldn't ask her to court, she really didn't' want to.

"I am glad to hear it." Isaac hesitated. He slowed the horse as he contemplated how to tell Martha the truth. "I have to ask you a question," he began.

"No!" Martha panicked and leapt from the still moving carriage. She fell to the ground and jumped up again, running across the field as fast as her legs would carry her. Isaac stopped the buggy and leapt out himself. He made to head off after her, but watched her dash into the fields where the buggy couldn't follow. He was perplexed. He didn't know what to do but he knew he couldn't go home and face his father without making sure Martha got home safely. He knew the direction she was heading and decided he would try to find her on the other side of the fields she was running through.

Martha ran and ran. She didn't know where she was going at first but she couldn't let Isaac ask her to court. She found herself running toward Hannah's barn and saw a light coming from inside. Could it be Eli, still working? She quickened her pace to a speed she didn't know she could do, her heart lifting her as she went.

She ran into the barn and there he was, tiding the place even though it looked immaculate.

Eli was wearing traditional Amish clothing, no hoody. She saw his scars on his face for an instant before he swung around so she couldn't see it. He looked both angry and concerned at the same time. When he saw that she was sweating and breathless he brought her a cloth and a drink of water.

"Are you ok?" he asked, now more concerned for Martha than embarrassed about his scars. Martha looked up at him and tried to smile. She could hardly catch her breath let alone respond to his question. Eli looked beyond Martha trying to figure out what she had been running from. He could see nothing.

"I'm fine," Martha managed to get out between pants. She took the water and the cloth from Eli. She drank the water in one thirsty gulp then mopped her dripping brow. She finally got control of her breathing. She looked into Eli's concerned face and laughed. "Don't look so worried, I'm fine Eli!"

"You remember me Martha?"

"Of course, Eli. I'm only upset that I did not recognize you yesterday. It is just that I wasn't really expecting to see you. You weren't the first person to come to mind. We played so much together in the past, as children. If I'm honest, I've have missed you." Martha smiled at the dark haired man that stood before her. He was not as tall as Isaac but he was every bit as muscular. His fine features made a handsome face despite the scars on his forehead and around his left eye. She noticed his arm and the scars that ran the length of it and down the back of his hand.

Eli noticed her looking and quickly rolled down his sleeve. Martha grabbed the hand that was rolling down the sleeve and stopped his frantic movement. "Does it hurt?" She asked as gently as she could.

"No, not any more," he said. He looked into her eyes and realized that she wasn't afraid, she wasn't repulsed. "Most people think I am ugly."

"You are handsome Eli Byler. Those scars are a gift that helps you remember your mother and your sister. I miss Elizabeth, but I still remember the fun we three had together." Martha said smiling at Eli.

"You are just as I remember you, kind and wise. You always say the right things at the right time Martha."

Martha straightened up. She suddenly felt her whole weight upon her and became embarrassed. "Ach, but I am not as I used to be. I am fat Eli Byler, and nobody likes a fat girl." She laughed to make light of her pain.

"Martha, how could anyone not like you. You are beautiful, both inside and out."

Suddenly they heard a buggy pull up in front of the barn."I have to go!" Martha exclaimed with a touch of fear and ran out the door leaving Eli to stare after her.

***

She was nearly home when it happened. Two strong arms seemed to come out of nowhere and grabbed Martha by the shoulders.

"Stop!" shouted Isaac. " What on earth are doing? I have to tell you something and you must hear me before it's too late." Martha was stunned by his words and stopped fighting. He released her shoulders and took a step back from her. "I am sorry I had to grab you, it was improper I just had to make you listen. I am sorry, you are a very nice person but I don't love you and I don't want to court you! There, I've said it."

Isaac was expecting tears and lots of them. Instead he was greeted by the widest smile he had ever seen. Martha laughed so hard she doubled over in two. Isaac was not expecting that. He didn't know what to do. This girl confused him more than anyone or anything ever had.

Martha confessed that she didn't want to be tied to Isaac either and she had been playing along to appease her mother. Isaac was so relieved that he started laughing as well.

"What are we going to do now?" Martha asked Isaac.

"I want to court Rebecca Miller but my father wants me to marry you. Your family has money, Rebecca's doesn't. He sees you as a way of insuring our family's future."

"Well," Martha said, "I have never been so insulted in my life. To be seen as a prize to be won!" Martha shook her head in disgust.

"I'm sorry Martha. He means well, he just doesn't understand. He thinks that I only like Rebecca because she is pretty, but I liked her before she became so pretty. We have been friends for many years and have talked often about our families and what we want from our future."

"Well then, we shall have to help you fulfill your dreams." Martha said. She dusted herself off and headed for her home down the drive. "Pick me up when your chores are done and we'll get to work." Martha shouted as she walked. Her step was buoyant and her spirits renewed. She would help Isaac Yoder and help herself in the process.

The next afternoon while Isaac was doing his chores, Jacob came to talk to him. "Have you asked Martha to court yet?"

"No, but I am going to see her after chores," Isaac answered honestly.

"I will finish your chores, you go and see Martha." Jacob offered a broad smile appearing on his thin face. He looked absolutely pleased that his plan was working.

Jacob grinned. Little did his father know that the tricking he was trying to play was about to fall apart. "Are you sure father? I am nearly done and can finish before I go."

"No, no, go and see that lovely girl of yours," Jacob was nearly giddy with joy.

Isaac almost felt guilty but he knew his father's motives were not pure and he should not waste guilt on them. Isaac quickly cleaned himself up and got the buggy ready. He was half way to Martha's house before he realized that he had no idea what she was planing.

Martha had been busy all morning. She had made a picnic to take out to the pond by Miller's farm. Thanks to Saloma she knew that Rebecca Miller would be out by the pond today. She had convinced her friend to bring Rebecca there and they would all have a look at the dress that Saloma had chosen for the dance. When Rebecca arrived she would help Isaac to ask her to accompany him for a picnic. Then she and Saloma would leave the two alone and they would go back to Saloma's house until it was time to head home. By the time the day was done Martha hoped that Isaac and Rebecca would be officially courting and she would be off the hook.

When Isaac arrived he brought the picnic basket out to the buggy and helped Martha climb in. They both smiled at Emma who was standing at the door smiling with glee.

"What did you tell your mother?" Isaac asked.

"All I had to tell her was that we are going for a picnic and she couldn't stop smiling the rest of the day."

Martha explained the plan to Isaac. He was excited but nervous. He thought he would have time to build up his courage and now he would have to ask right away. "Help me Martha, what should I say to Rebecca?" He asked nervously.

Martha laughed. "You are such a big strong man and you don't know how to ask a girl to court? Maybe your father was right? You do need to secure your future." She laughed again. Isaac frowned at her and hurried the horse. She suddenly understood that Isaac wasn't as confident as she thought. "I am sorry Isaac, I didn't mean it. I am just surprised that you would be so nervous, you always seem so self-assured."

"I am nervous because I want Rebecca to say yes and I don't know if she will," Isaac stammered.

Martha smiled tenderly at him. "I know that Rebecca will say yes. I spoke to Saloma this morning and she told me that Rebecca has been waiting for you to ask her for months. She is beginning to wonder if you ever would ask her."

Relief flooded through Isaac. Finally new knew that Rebecca liked him as well. "Thank you Martha, you are a great friend!"

He quickened the horse again, this time to hasten his proposal.

***

When they got to the pond Isaac and Martha set up the picnic. Rebecca and Saloma hadn't arrived yet so they decided to sit on the blanket and enjoy the sunshine. It was a beautiful day filled with so much hope. They talked and laughed together, teasing one another about the games they had played the night before and the silliness of each other's parents.

Passing on the road out of sight of the couple was a figure in a dark hoody. The scarred face contorted into a grimace and the slow walk turned into a run. Eli felt betrayed. He saw that Martha had taken up with a man. She was laughing with him and flirting. He knew he had no right to feel this way but he thought that Gott had brought her back into his life to make his transition easier. He ran past two girls who were laughing together. They said hello but he just ran faster, away from the pain in his heart.

Saloma was surprised to see Isaac waiting with Martha, but then it all began to make sense. "So Martha, you have wanted to see my dress so badly, and with Rebecca for a second opinion?"

Martha laughed, "Yes but I think we should look at it back at it in better light. Rebecca, why don't you stay and keep Isaac company while Saloma and I look for better light?" The pair laughed at the obvious rouse. Saloma and Martha went back up to the road and Martha noticed the boy in the hoody far ahead. "That's Eli." Martha said.

Saloma shrugged. "He is a rude Englischer. He ran past us and didn't say hello when we spoke to him."

"That doesn't sound like Eli. He is not Englischer either he is Amish. Don't you remember years ago when that family had their house burn down? The mother and twin sister were lost?"

"Ach, Jah that is the boy?" Saloma asked thoughtfully.

"Jah!"

"Well he seemed upset. We saw him walking until he looked over at the pond. He then pulled down his hood and started running."

"He looked at the pond?" Martha asked her friend, putting the pieces together.

"Jah, and then he started running down the road."

"Do you have your buggy hitched up?" Martha asked with a touch of panic in her voice.

"Why would I have my buggy ready? We were supposed to be looking at my dress, remember?" Saloma said tauntingly.

"I have to get home," Martha said and ran off toward her own house. She had to get to Eli and explain what had happened. She hoped that he would understand.

Eli arrived at his Aunt's house and quickly packed his bag. He was glad that no one was home. He scribbled a quick note explaining that he was going back to Chicago and that he would write to her when he got home. By the time he got on the road it was already approaching dusk. He pulled the hoody down and exposed his face to the last rays of the sun. He had barely spoken to Martha since his return and yet he felt so hurt by her. He knew she had done nothing wrong. He shouldn't have presumed that she would not be courting, but he had hoped. He had prayed for guidance as to his decision to stay in the community or go back to the Englisch world. He thought that Martha was his answer. He felt so rejected. Eli was so upset and deep in thought and didn't see the buggy charging toward him at breakneck speed until it was nearly on top of him. At the very last second he jumped out of the way and fell into the ditch with a loud thud.

Martha didn't see the figure until it jumped. The dark clothes Eli was wearing hid him in the shadows of the dusk. When she realized what she had done she pulled back on the reigns and brought the horse to a halt. She leapt from the buggy and ran back to where he had fallen and dropped to his side.

"Are you alright? I'm so sorry, I didn't see you…." she exclaimed, breathless and afraid she had hurt him.

"I'm fine!" Eli exclaimed, anger filling him. He yelled at her and cursed her for not being the gift from Gott he thought she was. He raged about his twin sister and his mother and how he had been stolen from the only home he ever knew. He didn't mean to let all this emotion out, but he couldn't stop it once it had begun. Martha took it all in, shocked by his fierceness but she understood his pain.

When he had run out of words he collapsed to the ground, tears rolling down his face, exhausted from the weight he had been carrying all those years. Martha put her hand on his shoulder.

"I'm sorry," she said simply, and waited for him to reply.

He lay silent for what felt "I'm sorry too. I shouldn't have dumped all that on you. I was just hoping for so much more when I came here."

"Like what?" Martha asked.

"I am embarrassed to say," Eli said.

"Please tell me."

"When you nearly ran me down the last time," he looked up at her and grinned, "I had been praying for a sign that I should stay in the community. I thought you were that sign."

"Why do you think I wasn't?" She looked into his eyes. He looked away.

"Because you are already taken. I am too late."

Martha laughed, "I was waiting with Isaac for Rebecca to arrive. I was helping him fix him up with her. Our parents wanted us to court but we are not interested in each other in that way." She smiled encouragingly as Eli turned to face her.

Eli smiled sheepishly at her. "I guess I look like a fool to you?"

"No, you look like my friend who has been returned to me. I am happy you are home and I hope you will stay."

The next day everything had been sorted out. Well almost everything. Isaac still hadn't asked Rebecca to court. Martha had gone to see him to find out how everything had gone and he told her that he had forgotten to ask her. They had had a wonderful time, he drove her home but it wasn't until he was halfway home that he realized that he had forgotten to ask Rebecca to court. Martha threw up her arms in frustration.

"How could you forget? It was the whole purpose of the day. Now what are we going to do?" She asked him rhetorically. She couldn't believe that the man had been such a fool. He had become so engulfed in enjoying their time together that he had actually forgotten to get confirmation that Rebecca would indeed agree to court him.

"There's always next Sunday," he said hopefully.

"No! We are not waiting that long. Come with me now!" She commanded. She need this matter closed. Her mother hadn't stopped asking about the picnic the previous day. She need to be able to explain everything once and for all.

"But my chores aren't done." Isaac protested.

"Should I tell your father that I will marry you?" She gave him a stern look.

He laughed and then realized that she was serious. "No, I will come now." He said. "You will make a fine mother one day. Your children will never disobey you."

She laughed as they made their way to the barn to get the carriage. Jacob was in the barn.

"Hello Martha!" He grinned at the young woman as if she were a prize goose.

"Hello Jacob. Do you mind if I borrow Isaac for a couple of hours?" she asked primly.

"No, you young folk go and have fun, enjoy each other's company," he smiled and gave them an encouraging wave. "Take your time Isaac."

"Thank you Daed. I will make up for it tomorrow," Isaac promised.

"No need, no need," Jacob winked at Isaac and carried on with his chores.

They got the buggy hooked up to the horse and headed out to the Miller's farm.

On the way they saw Eli walking down the road. Martha asked Isaac to slow down.

"You are always walking down the road Eli." Martha said to her friend.

"At least you didn't run me down this time." Eli laughed.

Isaac cocked his head not understanding their private joke.

Martha introduced the two men and told them the missing details of each other's story. They laughed at the absurdity of the situation they all found themselves in. Isaac invited Eli to join them on their trip to the Miller's farm and Eli gladly accepted. As they road along memories came flooding back to Eli. He remembered his family riding along in their buggy many years ago. It had felt like a different lifetime. He remembered playing with Elizabeth and bouncing baby Mary on his knee while his parents talked. They were wonderful days and for the first time he didn't feel sad remembering the joy they had shared as a family. He sat back in the carriage and smiled. It suddenly hit him that the entire time he had been back in the community, no one, not even Isaac just now, had reacted with anything other than compassion in regards to his situation. No one had made any comment about his face or appearance either.

That was the moment that Eli Byler was home.

It didn't matter what happened now. He would be baptized and work hard to buy a farm. He hoped to take Martha as his wife and they would live together happily for the rest of their lives. He thought all of these thoughts in the moments between his joyful praises to Gott. He thanked Gott for the sign he had been looking for and the elation he felt in his heart for the first time since he was a child.

They arrived at the Miller's farm and bundled out of the buggy. The trio approached the house and was greeted by Rebecca and her mother.

"Good morning young ones, "Rebecca's mother said, "could I offer you some kaffe and pie?" She smiled at her daughter hoping that this time Isaac Yoder would find the courage to ask Rebecca to court.

"That would be very nice of you Ruth," Isaac said.

They all went into the house and Ruth made them coffee and served pie. She made her excuses as soon as they all had settled down and went back out to the barn. They chatted for several minutes. Martha introduced Rebecca and Eli and they talked about Eli's choice to be baptized. Eli and Martha kept trying to nudge Isaac to ask Rebecca. Isaac blushed and shook his head.

"Rebecca, Isaac wants to ask you something. He has wanted to ask you for a long time, but it is hard for him," Eli said taking control of the situation.

"He is shy, but only because it means so much to him." Martha added.

Isaac was growing more embarrassed with the help his friends were giving him. He burst out with "Rebecca will you marry me?" Before he realized what he had said. He looked shocked and anxious.

Rebecca laughed. "You don't want to court first?"

"If you would prefer to court first we can do that." He tried to save himself from the mistake he had made.

"Jah, I would love to marry you Isaac Yoder. Maybe it is best that we don't waste anymore time?" She gave him a look that made Isaac love her even more.

Eli and Martha decided to walk home to give the pair at least a few moments together. Isaac was clearly relieved and Rebecca was happy that it was finally happening.

"Martha?" Eli asked.

"Jah?"

"I was too young to know the proper way of doing these things but would you be my girlfriend?"

Martha laughed. She was familiar with the Englisch term but she had never heard it put just that way. "Yes, Eli Byler, I will be your girlfriend."

Eli went to take Martha's hand, but wasn't sure if it was appropriate so he put his hand in his pocket hoping she hadn't noticed his uncertainty. She did and she smiled at him. Soon Eli you will remember everything you have forgotten. They walked together basking in the light of hope and Gott's love.

A month later Eli Byler was baptized and accepted back into the community he had been taken from in childhood. The whole community had welcomed him with open arms. They saw in him the little boy he was and the earnest man he had become. They recognized that he was committed to the Amish ways; they had never really left him. His commitment to Gott was stronger than most people his age. He had been through so much and it had given him an unbreakable faith.

Eli and Martha had been courting for a just a month when he asked her to marry him. They had decided to wait until the next marriage season to actually wed because Eli wanted to give her a home that he had provided. He asked her the evening of his baptism and she didn't hesitate to say yes. They knew that their coming together was Gott's will and were overjoyed to have been so blessed.

Isaac and Rebecca were married a month after Eli's Baptism. Eli and Martha obviously attended the wedding and were given the credit for getting the couple together at last. Jacob wasn't very happy when he first learned that he had been deceived by his son, but he soon relented when he realized how happy Rebecca made the boy. By the time the wedding happened anyone would have thought that Jacob had planned the match from the beginning.

Emma on the other hand was convinced the moment she met Eli. Martha had brought him home the day that Isaac had proposed to Rebecca.

"Mamm, I want you to meet Eli Byler," she said.

Emma took one look at the boy with the scarred face and felt her heart fill with love for the boy. She saw in his eyes the pure hope that she would accept him and her eyes filled with tears. She quickly hugged the boy and begged his forgiveness for her calling him an Englischer.

"I never heard you call me that but I guess I kind of am," he agreed.

"You never were!" Emma chastised and smiled at the sweet boy. She brought him in and fed him, her way of showing love.

They had had a wonderful afternoon together and then Martha told her mother about Eli and her courting. Emma was very pleased for them.

"What about Jacob?" Martha teased.

"He will have to find another trough to drink from," Emma laughed. She was too happy for her daughter to think on such trivial things.

As months moved steadily forward Eli went to work. He was able to buy a farm, thanks largely to Emma who found him a piece of land and negotiated a price that he could afford. He wasn't expecting to have land so quickly but he was grateful for Emma's persistence. Eli bought animals and got the farm ready to build a new life with Martha. Isaac helped him as much as he could, mentoring the younger man and getting him prepared for all the rigors of Amish life. The two had become best friends and Isaac taught Eli manner of farming techniques.

Eli's father, step-mother and sister came for a visit but only stayed a short time His father approved of the farm he had bought and liked the Kings very much, but the whole visit brought back many bad memories. His father was unsure how to act. Had he been shunned? Did those that remember him understand? Eli's sister, Mary was different. She decided that she wanted to come back and stay for the summer. She had begun to remember her early childhood and the life she had lived in this loving community.

Mary did come for the summer, and never left. She was baptized a few weeks before Martha and Eli were married. She came and lived with them and learned the Amish ways from her new sister-in-law. Emma took great pleasure in teaching Mary how to cook, bake and sew. She came over to the farm and worked with the girls every day she could. Before long Martha was pregnant.

As the years lapped ahead of the happy couple their family grew to six children. Emma eventually moved into the farm house and Mary was married to a fine gentleman and had children of her own. Eli's father never returned to the community, not even for a visit. He never met his grand children. He wrote letters and told his children that it was just too painful to be there. The family always remembered him in their prayers and hoped that Gott could forgive him.

Martha and Eli had felt like outcasts until they found each other. When they had come together they stopped seeing their own faults and blemishes and saw only beauty in themselves and the world Gott had provided for them. The love they had for one another and for their family was an example to all who met them.

I would like to thank you for taking the time to read my book. I really hope that you enjoyed it as much as I enjoyed writing it.

I have been writing Amish books for Amazon for almost two years now, almost exclusively on Kindle. However, due to growing demand I managed to get the majority of my titles available in paperback versions. There is a list of all of my kindle books below, bit by bit they are ALL going to be released in paperback so please keep checking them.

If you feel able I would love for you to give the book a short review on Amazon.

If you want to keep up to date with all of my latest releases then please like my Facebook Page, simply search for Hannah Schrock author.

Many thanks once again, all my love.

Hannah.

LATEST BOOKS

DON'T MISS HANNAH'S BRAND NEW *MAMMOTH AMISH MEGA BOOK* - 20 Stories in one box set.

Mammoth Amish Romance Mega Book 20 books in one set

Outstanding value for 20 books

OTHER BOX SETS

Amish Romance Mega book (contains many of Hannah's older titles)

Amish Love and Romance Collection

MOST RECENT SINGLE TITLES

The Orphan's Amish Teacher

The Mysterious Amish Suicide

The Pregnant Amish Quilt Maker

The Amish Caregiver

The Amish Detective: The King Family Arsonist

The Amish Gift

Becoming Amish

The Amish Foundling Girl

The Heartbroken Amish Girl

The Missing Amish Girl

Amish Joy

The Amish Detective

Amish Double

The Burnt Amish Girl

AMISH ROMANCE SERIES

AMISH HEARTACHE

AMISH REFLECTIONS: AMISH ANTHOLOGY COLLECTION

MORE AMISH REFLECTIONS : ANOTHER AMISH ANTHOLOGY COLLECTION

THE AMISH WIDOW AND THE PREACHER'S SON

AN AMISH CHRISTMAS WITH THE BONTRAGER SISTERS

A BIG BEAUTIFUL AMISH COURTSHIP

AMISH YOUNG SPRING LOVE BOX SET

AMISH PARABLES SERIES BOX SET

AMISH HEART SHORT STORY COLLECTION

AMISH HOLDUP

AN AMISH TRILOGY BOX SET

AMISH ANGUISH

SHORT AMISH ROMANCE STORIES

AMISH BONTRAGER SISTERS 2 - THE COMPLETE SECOND SEASON

AMISH BONTRAGER SISTERS - THE COMPLETE FIRST SEASON

THE AMISH BROTHER'S BATTLE

AMISH OUTSIDER

AMISH FORGIVENESS AND FRIENDSHIP

THE AMISH OUTSIDER'S LIE

AMISH VANITY

AMISH NORTH

AMISH YOUNG SPRING LOVE SHORT STORIES SERIES

THE AMISH BISHOP'S DAUGHTER

AN AMISH ARRANGEMENT

AMISH REJECTION

AMISH BETRAYAL

THE AMISH BONTRAGER SISTERS SHORT STORIES SERIES

AMISH RETURN

AMISH BONTRAGER SISTERS COMPLETE COLLECTION

AMISH APOLOGY

AMISH UNITY

AMISH DOUBT

AMISH FAMILY

THE ENGLISCHER'S GIFT

AMISH SECRET

AMISH PAIN

THE AMISH PARABLES SERIES

THE AMISH BUILDER

THE AMISH PRODIGAL SON

AMISH PERSISTENCE

THE AMISH GOOD SAMARITAN

Manufactured by Amazon.ca
Bolton, ON

38203934R00022